Copyright © 2022 by The Pr...

All rights reserved. No part of this book may...
manner without prior written permissio...
except for the use of quotations in a book review.

ISBN: 9798415424702

Imprint: Independently published

Contents Page

Introduction	1
John Barnes	3
Ian Callaghan	6
Jamie Carragher	9
Ray Clemence	12
Kenny Dalglish	15
Robbie Fowler	18
Steven Gerrard	21
Bruce Grobbelaar	24
Alan Hansen	27
Emlyn Hughes	30
Roger Hunt	33
Kevin Keegan	36
Ray Kennedy	39
Billy Liddell	42
Terry McDermott	45
Steve McManaman	48
Phil Neal	51
Michael Owen	54
Bob Paisley	57
Ian Rush	60
Tommy Smith	63
Graeme Souness	67
Luis Suárez	70
Phil Thompson	73
Fernando Torres	76

Introduction

Welcome to the Liverpool Biographies for Kids. I hope you're raring to learn about 25 legends of this amazing football club!

Each player's biography will start with a full-size image so that you are able to recognise them in future if you don't already! This will be followed by two pages of information starting with a few stats which are date of birth, year of Liverpool debut, nationality, position, height and major trophies won during their time at the club (including Charity Shields and Super Cups).

Next, you'll get an overview of their early career, late career, accomplishments and a summary with a particular focus on their Anfield careers. Enjoy!

Trophy Cabinet

First Division/Premier League (19)
1900–01, 1905–06, 1921–22, 1922–23, 1946–47, 1963–64, 1965–66, 1972–73, 1975–76, 1976–77, 1978–79, 1979–80, 1981–82, 1982–83, 1983–84, 1985–86, 1987–88, 1989–90, 2019–20

Second Division (4)
1893–94, 1895–96, 1904–05, 1961–62

FA Cup (7)
1964–65, 1973–74, 1985–86, 1988–89, 1991–92, 2000–01, 2005–06

League Cup (9)
1980–81, 1981–82, 1982–83, 1983–84, 1994–95, 2000–01, 2002–03, 2011–12, 2021–22

Charity Shield (15)
1964*, 1965*, 1966, 1974, 1976, 1977*, 1979, 1980, 1982, 1986*, 1988, 1989, 1990*, 2001, 2006 (* shared)

European Cup/Champions League (6)
1976–77, 1977–78, 1980–81, 1983–84, 2004–05, 2018–19

UEFA Cup (3)
1972–73, 1975–76, 2000–01

UEFA Super Cup (4)
1977, 2001, 2005, 2019

FIFA Club World Cup (1)
2019

JOHN BARNES

Born: 7th November 1963
Liverpool Debut: 1987
Nationality: English
Position: Left Winger/Midfielder
Height: 5 ft 11 in (1.81 m)
Major Trophies: 8

Early Career

John Charles Bryan Barnes was born in Kingston, Jamaica, to parents of West Indian origin. After spending time at a military base, the family moved to London in 1976 whilst he was 12, where Barnes played competitive youth football whilst at school. He signed for Watford in 1981 and made his debut aged just 17, swiftly becoming a regular member of the team, as Watford returned to the First Division. They would go on to finish second to Liverpool the following season and come runners up to Everton in the 1984 FA Cup Final. Barnes would eventually go on to sign for Liverpool in 1987, leaving the team for whom he played 233 league games and scored 65 times. He debuted for Liverpool in August 1987 and scored his first goal a month later.

Later Career

In his first season with the club, Barnes chalked up 15 league goals, as Liverpool won the First Division championship. During that season Barnes was instrumental in Liverpool's 5-0 home win over Forest described by Tom Finney as "One of the finest exhibitions I've seen the whole time I've played and watched the game. You couldn't see it bettered anywhere, not even in Brazil." With that he attained the PFA Player of the Year award. He missed an England game to attend funerals of those killed in the Hillsborough disaster in 1989. His skills and creativity helped defeat Everton in the FA Cup Final, and he posted a career-best 22 league goals in the following campaign as Liverpool again won the title in 1990. Injuries blighted him for the next few seasons but he did captain the side for a period in the 1995/96 season. In August 1997, after ten years at Liverpool, he left the club on a free transfer. He was taken on by Newcastle United who were managed by Kenny Dalglish and was their top scorer in his debut season. Change in personnel at the club saw Barnes demoted to the reserves, and he left to join Charlton Athletic in February 1999. After a brief spell at the club, Barnes decided to retire after 20 years as a player. He then took up football management and had short spells at Celtic, Tranmere Rovers and the Jamaica national team.

Accomplishments

In 407 appearances for Liverpool, Barnes scored 108 goals, and in his whole career played 751 times netting 198 goals. In that time, he won two First Division titles, one FA Cup, and one League Cup. He was inducted into the English Football Hall of Fame in 2005 and was honoured with an MBE in 1998, while still playing. For the England national side, he scored 11 times in 79 outings. Off the pitch, he performed a series of raps in a few football songs that spent a number of weeks in the UK music singles charts.

Summary: John Barnes has been praised for his speed and dribbling skills throughout his long career. He was able to attack defences and create openings for other players. He currently works as a pundit on television, having also appeared on several celebrity television programmes.

IAN CALLAGHAN

Born: 10th April 1942
Liverpool Debut: 1960
Nationality: English
Position: Midfielder
Height: 5ft 7in (1.70m)
Major Trophies: 17

Early Career

Born in the inner-city area of Liverpool, Toxteth, Ian Robert Callaghan started playing schoolboy football in his hometown, before joining Liverpool as an apprentice in 1957. He made his first-team debut in April 1960 aged only 18 and got his first goal in November 1961. After Liverpool won promotion back to the First Division in 1962/63, Callaghan started to get a regular team place and began his early days as a winger providing service for the front two strikers. He played in all 42 league games in 1963/64 as Liverpool won the First Division title for the first time since 1946/47.

Later Career

He provided the cross for the winning goal in the 1965 FA Cup final, and he played another full league season in 1965/66 as Liverpool won a record-equalling seventh title and reached the final of the European Cup Winners' Cup. Callaghan scored eight goals during the 1968/69 season, a joint career-best, but needed a knee operation during the 1970/71 campaign. When he returned to the team, he was moved to the central midfield position, where he excelled for a few more years. Liverpool got back to their winning ways in 1972/73, with Callaghan once again playing a full season. It included a run of 21 home wins in a row, and a triumph in the UEFA Cup. In August,

Callaghan broke the record for the most appearances by a Liverpool player. Further success followed for Callaghan before his final season in 1977/78; two consecutive First Division League titles, two consecutive European Cup triumphs, an FA Cup, and a UEFA Cup. Callaghan played his final game in a Liverpool shirt on the 29th of March 1978. He later played in the US, Australia, Ireland, Wales and finally for Crewe Alexandra. The final game in his long and illustrious career came in the 1981/82 season playing in the fourth tier at the age of 40.

Accomplishments

Callaghan made a record 857 appearances for Liverpool in 19 seasons, over 100 games more than the second-best placed player. This included 640 League matches, another club record scoring 68 goals in all competitions. During his long career, he won five First Division titles, two FA Cups, two European Cups, two UEFA Cups, and one Second Division title. He amassed 979 football games in total in his career. He played four times for the England national team and was part of the squad that won the 1966 World Cup. He received a winner's medal in 2009, having not participated in the final. The gap between his second and third cap was 11 years 49 days - a national record of time between two caps for any England player.

Summary: Ian Callaghan was one of the great wingers and later midfield players to play for Liverpool, emphasised by the number of games he played. He received an MBE in 1975 while still playing for Liverpool, and he had the enviable record of having been booked only once in his career. After retirement he set up his own business.

JAMIE CARRAGHER

Born: 28th January 1978
Liverpool Debut: 1996
Nationality: English
Position: Defender
Height: 6 ft 1 in (1.85 m)
Major Trophies: 11

Early Career

Born in the town of Bootle, Merseyside, James Lee Duncan Carragher signed for Liverpool's youth team at the age 10 and regularly attended training in his Graeme Sharp Everton shirt having supported the club in his youth. Carragher's father was also an Everton supporter, and his two middle names (Lee Duncan) are a tribute to Gordon Lee and Duncan McKenzie. He made his professional debut in January 1997 and scored his first goal ten days later. He became more of a regular the following season. He played a mainly defensive midfield role in his early days and was named the club's Player of the Year in 1998/99, having played 44 games. He also won over 30 caps for England at youth level.

Later Career

Carragher played at left-back in 2000/01, as Liverpool triumphed in five competitions, including the FA Cup and the UEFA Cup, before being hit by two major injuries, one of which caused him to miss the 2002 World Cup. A move to the centre-half position in 2004/05 transformed his career, his role proving crucial in Liverpool's 2005 Champions League triumph. He received a nomination for the 2005 Ballon d'Or, an award given to the best footballer in Europe. In 2006, he scored his first league goal in over seven years, only his fourth in a Liverpool shirt. The same year he helped Liverpool win the FA Cup

Final against West Ham in Cardiff, despite scoring an own goal. He temporarily retired from international football in 2006, but he soon made his 500th appearance for the club. A charity fund-raising testimonial was set up in 2010 in his honour, and five months later he set the record for the most appearances by a British footballer in European club competition. When he retired in May 2013, he had donned the Liverpool shirt in over 500 league games and become the second-highest in the list of club appearances by an individual with a colossal 737 games.

Accomplishments

Playing for Liverpool, Carragher won the FA Cup twice, the Champions League once, the UEFA Cup once, the League Cup three times, and the FA Youth Cup in his younger days. He participated in 508 league games, scoring just four goals, and 737 in total with five goals. He played for the England national side 38 times between 1999 and 2010. Carragher continues to support various charity projects since retiring as a player, including helping the young and the homeless. He also participated in a charity match in aid of UNICEF.
 He won 38 caps for England, playing at two World Cups and a European Championship. He is currently with Sky Sports working as a football pundit, having worked there for a number of years, and has also worked for other media outlets, including popular newspapers, radio, and Danish television.

Summary: Jamie Carragher played all his 17 years at Liverpool, and became one of the best defenders around, even though he supported their Merseyside rivals, Everton, when he was young. His success came in that position, having played in midfield earlier in his career. A tough and durable opponent, he showed great stamina and versatility. He won Liverpool's player of the year three times.

RAY CLEMENCE

Born: 5th August 1948
Liverpool Debut: 1968
Nationality: English
Position: Goalkeeper
Height: 6 ft 0 in (1.83 m)
Major Trophies: 18

Early Career

Raymond Neal Clemence was born in the seaside town of Skegness, Lincolnshire. He competed for his local youth club and was signed by Third Division Scunthorpe United in 1965, having already had trials with Notts County. He made his debut in April 1966 aged 17 and spent his first season in the reserves. He eventually became their first-choice 'keeper in 1966/67, appearing in 46 consecutive matches, adding up to 50 appearances, and 12 clean sheets. At this time, Liverpool became interested in the young goalkeeper and proceeded to sign Clemence in June 1967 for a fee of £18,000. Initially, a reserve team player, he eventually became their number one keeper in 1970.

Later Career

Clemence saw success in 1973, scooping up the League title and UEFA Cup - where his penalty save in the first leg of the final proved crucial to Liverpool winning the competition. The same double was achieved in 1976, before the club came out victorious in the European Cup for the first time in 1977, with Clemence again pulling off a vital save in the final with the game finely poised. He kept a clean sheet as Liverpool retained the European Cup against Belgian side Brugge and set a record during the 1978/79 season by only conceding 16 goals in 42 league games, including only four at home, and keeping 28 clean sheets, a personal best. Clemence tasted victory again in 1981, when Liverpool claimed the League Cup and the European Cup. The 1-0 defeat of Real Madrid on May 27th turned out to be his final game for the club. During the final 11 seasons with the team, Clemence only missed six matches. The emergence of Bruce Grobbelaar put Clemence's place in the side under threat and he subsequently joined Tottenham Hotspur in 1981 for £300,00. He won the 1982 FA Cup before joining a select group of players to play in five or more FA Cup Finals in 1987. He retired in 1988 and joined Sprus' coaching staff shortly after.

Accomplishments

Clemence spent 14 seasons at Liverpool and played in 665 matches, with 470 of them in the league, 54 in the FA Cup, and 80 in Europe. From 1970 to 1981 he participated in six full league seasons out of 11. He kept a total of 323 clean sheets, including 226 in the league. He won five League titles, three European Cups, one FA Cup, two UEFA Cups, and one League Cup. With Tottenham, he achieved an FA Cup and a UEFA Cup triumph. For the England national team, Clemence appeared in 61 matches between 1972 and 1983. He was awarded an MBE in 1987 for his services to football, and his son made over 200 Premier League appearances for Spurs and Birmingham City.

Summary: Ray Clemence was one of the best goalkeepers to ever play in the English football league and was also one of the most reliable. After retiring he coached for a while with Tottenham Hotspur, before joining the England national football team as goalkeeping coach. He passed away in November 2020.

KENNY DALGLISH

Born: 4th March 1951
Liverpool Debut: 1977
Nationality: Scottish
Position: Forward
Height: 5 ft 8 in (1.73 m)
Major Trophies: 20

Early Career

Kenneth Mathieson Dalglish was born in the city of Glasgow, Scotland. His family moved near to the home ground of Scottish side Rangers, whom he supported. He played for the national schoolboys team before he signed his first major contract with Celtic in May 1967. Starting off mainly playing for the reserve team, Dalglish made his first team debut in September 1968 and scored his first goal in August 1971. Now a regular, he scored 29 goals in 53 matches during the 1971/72 season, helping the team to win its seventh successive league title. Further success followed with goals and trophies aplenty, including three league titles before moving south of the border to Liverpool. He was signed in August 1977 for a British record transfer fee of £440,000. In nine seasons with Celtic, Dalglish played 338 games and scored 173 goals.

Later Career

Dalglish made himself at home with his new club, scoring a goal on his league debut in August, and then the winner against Bruges in the 1978 European Cup final, ending his first season with 31 goals in 62 matches. The second season saw him net a career-best 21 league goals for the club, and being a regular in the team, saw him continue his consistent goal scoring as Liverpool won four league titles in five years. He became a player-manager for the 1985/86 season and helped his side to win the double, the FA Cup and the League, personally scoring the goal that secured the club's 16th championship title. He played just three league matches in his final three years as a player to focus on managerial duties and eventually played his final match in May 1990 at the age of 39. His last goal had come in 1987. In the 13 seasons he had been there, Liverpool won an amazing six First Division League titles, three European Cups, one FA Cup, and four League Cups.

Accomplishments

Dalglish played a total of 515 matches for Liverpool scoring 172 goals. He was the Ballon d'Or runner-up in 1983 and inducted into both the English and Scottish Football Halls of Fame. For Celtic, Dalglish won the Scottish championship four times, the Scottish Cup four times, and the League Cup once. After resigning as Liverpool manager in 1991 he joined Blackburn Rovers where he won the 1994/95 Premier League title on the final day at Anfield. He then managed Newcastle and Celtic before a second spell at Liverpool where he won the 2012 League Cup. For Scotland, Dalglish appeared in a record 102 matches, and scored a joint-record 30 goals. He was awarded an MBE in 1985 for his services to football and honoured with the title 'Sir' in 2018 after becoming a Knight Bachelor. The centenary stand at Anfield was named in his honour in May 2017.

Summary: Kenny Dalglish had a remarkable career with both Liverpool and Celtic, winning countless major titles, and becoming a legend in the world of football. He played mainly as a forward and scored regularly throughout his career. Due to his success at Anfield, he earned the nickname 'King Kenny'. He set up his own cancer charity in 2004.

ROBBIE FOWLER

Born: 9th April 1975
Liverpool Debut: 1993
Nationality: English
Position: Striker
Height: 5 ft 9 in (1.75 m)
Major Trophies: 5

Early Career

Robert Bernard Fowler was born in the Toxteth area of Liverpool. Like numerous academy graduates, he was a supporter of rivals Everton. He starred for his schoolboy team on a regular basis, once scoring 16 times in a game. After leaving school he signed for Liverpool playing for the youth team, before going on to become a professional with them in April 1992, aged just 17. He scored on his debut in a cup tie in September 1993, before scoring an incredible five goals in the return leg two weeks later. He notched his first league hat-trick in only his fifth game, and by the time he had played 13 matches he had already scored 12 goals. During this time, he also made his debut for the England Under-21 team.

Later Career

He became a regular during the 1994/95 season, competing in all 57 matches, and against Arsenal in August completed the fastest ever hat-trick in Premier League history in four minutes and 33 seconds. This record stood for 20 years until it was beaten by Sadio Mané. He was chosen as the PFA Young Player of the Year, an accolade he also won the following season in 1996. By December 1996, he had scored 100 goals for Liverpool in only 165 matches, when he slotted home four goals in one game against Middlesbrough. He recorded 30 or more goals in three successive seasons. Fowler had a memorable 2000/01 season, scoring 17 goals, winning three trophies, appearing in three cup finals, and being a captain for the team. He contributed towards all three cup competition victories and held the winning trophy aloft on all three occasions. Internal problems then led to Fowler being linked with other clubs, and he moved to Leeds United in November 2001. After a short time, he was transferred to Manchester City, but the goals almost dried up. He scored his 150th Premier League goal in 2005, and despite an improvement in scoring, injury problems started to occur. He decided another move was needed and he returned to Anfield in 2006. The goals continued but at a less prolific rate, and with limited starts played his last game for the club on May 13th, 2007. Fowler would go on to play for Cardiff City and Blackburn Rovers, together with two short stints in Australia. He also went on to manage football teams in Thailand, Australia, and India.

Accomplishments

Fowler's Liverpool career lasted for 11 seasons, playing in 369 games scoring 183 goals, including 128 league goals in 266 matches. During his career, he made 590 appearances and scored 254 times. His main achievements included winning the FA Cup, the UEFA Cup, and the League Cup twice. He also scored 7 goals in 26 caps for England.

Summary: A prolific goal-scorer, Fowler was a quick and opportunistic striker, with good technical ability and a reputation as a poacher. His prime was undoubtedly in the 1990s before he began to become more injury-prone later in his career. He earned the nickname "God" from the Anfield fans and he remains Liverpool's top scorer in the Premier League.

STEVEN GERRARD

Born: 30th May 1980
Liverpool Debut: 1998
Nationality: English
Position: Midfielder
Height: 6 ft 1 in (1.85 m)
Major Trophies: 9

Early Career

Steven George Gerrard was born in the town of Whiston, Merseyside, and started playing for the local team Whiston Juniors, before joining the Liverpool youth team at age 9. He signed a professional contract with Liverpool and made his debut in 1998 but made minimal appearances. He scored his first goal in December 1999. The 2000/01 season saw Gerrard play in 50 matches, and also win his first major titles with the club; the UEFA Cup, the FA Cup, and the League Cup. He was honoured with the PFA Young Player of the Year award.

Later Career

More success followed, with Gerrard scoring in the 2-0 win over Manchester United in the 2003 League Cup final. This led to the captaincy post in October 2003, having served as a vice-captain. Gerrard netted a stunning goal to help Liverpool make the knockout stages of the 2005 Champions League, where they beat AC Milan on penalties in the final where he was named Man of the Match. The 2005/06 season saw Gerrard score 23 goals in 53 games, receiving the prestigious PFA Players' Player of the Year award at the end of the season. Liverpool won their second successive major trophy on penalties, when they triumphed in the 2006 FA Cup final with Gerrard the hero, having scored the crucial equaliser to send the match into extra time. In between, he came sixth in the running for the FIFA World Player of the year. His 100th goal for the club came in October 2008, before netting his first Premier League hat-trick in March 2009. Injuries blighted him in the next couple of seasons before a memorable match took place in March 2012. He scored a hat-trick in the Merseyside Derby in his 400th Premier League appearance as his side beat Everton 3-0. A testimonial fund-raising match was awarded to Gerrard in August 2013, before becoming the first player from the club to score in 15 consecutive seasons, and the longest-serving club captain after ten years in the post. A 100th Premier League goal was chalked up in October 2013, before helping his side to second place in the league. He played his final game for the club on May 24th 2015. Gerrard spent two seasons with US Major League Soccer side LA Galaxy, before making his final professional football appearance in November 2016, aged 36. His first managerial job was at Rangers before joining Aston Villa in 2021.

Accomplishments

With Liverpool, Gerrard won the Champions League once, the FA Cup twice, the League Cup three times, and the UEFA Cup once. He played in 504 Premier League games, scoring 120 goals. In total, he played 710 games and scored 186 times for Liverpool. He played for England from 2000 to 2014, appearing 114 times with 21 goals including six major tournaments. He captained England 38 times. He was manager of Scottish side Rangers, leading them to the 2020/21 title, their first in a decade. He earned an MBE in 2007.

Summary: Stevie G was one of the greatest players of his generation. He was a classic box-to-box midfielder and an attacking threat with his famous long-range goals known for his loyalty to the club.

BRUCE GROBBELAAR

Born: 6th October 1957
Liverpool Debut: 1981
Nationality: Zimbabwean
Position: Goalkeeper
Height: 6 ft 1 in (1.85 m)
Major Trophies: 19

Early Career

Bruce David Grobbelaar was born in Durban, South Africa, but moved to Rhodesia (now Zimbabwe) when only two months old. He played for a football team based in Bulawayo, before being called up by the army. He signed for the North American team, Vancouver Whitecaps in 1978, before a visit to England saw him being recruited by Crewe Alexandra. He played a few games on loan and even scored what turned out to be his sole career goal. Soon after, First Division side Liverpool expressed their interest when he went back to Vancouver. They paid £250,000 to secure his signature in March 1981 and soon made the number one shirt his own after Ray Clemence's move to Tottenham. He kept his first clean sheet a week after making his debut in late August, and despite early struggles, picked up a League championship and League Cup medal.

Later Career

From the time of his debut, Grobbelaar played in 317 consecutive games for the club, including every league game in his first five seasons of playing. In that time Liverpool secured nine major trophies, including four League titles, one European Cup, one FA Cup, and three League Cup. He kept over 30 clean sheets in each of the next two seasons. In the 1984 European Cup final, Grobbelaar produced his famous 'wobbling legs' as Liverpool came out victorious in the penalty shootout against Roma. He played his 200th game just after the start of the 1984/85 season, only three years after his debut. Grobbelaar was retained by three of Liverpool's greatest managers; Paisley, Fagan and Dalglish, over a period of 13 years which is a testament to his ability and consistency. The arrival of youngster David James limited his game time in the 1992/93 season but he gained his place back the following season. After leaving Liverpool in 1994 he made over 40 appearances each for Southampton and Plymouth Argyle before playing sporadically for nine other clubs.

Accomplishments

In 13 seasons with Liverpool, Grobbelaar won six League championships, one European Cup, three FA Cups, three League Cups, and five Charity Shields. He played in 628 games, with 440 of them in the league. In over 30 years of senior football, he played for 19 different teams, in over 780 games. He played 32 times for Zimbabwe.

Summary: Bruce Grobbelaar was one of the most eccentric and colourful characters to play the game. Agility, confidence, and flair were just some of the components which kept him at the top of his game at Liverpool. He coached teams in South Africa, North America, Norway, and Zimbabwe. He participated in a hit song and wrote an autobiography. In 1994, he was involved in match-fixing allegations which badly affected his game.

ALAN HANSEN

Born: 13th June 1955
Liverpool Debut: 1977
Nationality: Scottish
Position: Centre Back/Defender
Height: 6 ft 2 in (1.88m)
Major Trophies: 25

Early Career

Alan David Hansen was born in the small town of Sauchie in Scotland and supported Rangers. At 15, he had a major head accident and started playing golf, before being tempted back into football two years later after passing up his place at the University of Aberdeen. He joined Partick Thistle where his brother was playing and won promotion to the top tier in 1975/76. Watched closely by Liverpool, he eventually joined the club in 1977. He notched his first goal a month after making his debut and played in the 1978 European Cup final against Brugge despite only playing 18 league games in his maiden season.

Later Career

Hansen made more regular appearances in the following season, as Liverpool won the league title with a record points tally and only four goals conceded at home. He became an automatic choice in central defence as the club won its second successive championship. More trophies were earned, with Hansen a constant presence in defence; six titles in three years. In 1983/84, with manager Bob Paisley having retired, Liverpool completed a treble of championships, including the League title and the European Cup. The infamous 1985 European Cup Final defeat to Juventus, now known as the Heysel disaster was his last European game for the club. Hansen played in all 42 league games and 67 in total throughout the season, his most while at the club. He captained the side during the 1987/88 campaign as Liverpool claimed the league title by losing just two games. Hansen was honoured with a testimonial match in May 1988 against an England XI, but was injured before the start of the 1988/89 season, though he did appear in the FA Cup Final victory. He skippered the club to another First Division title in 1989/90 making it a record-breaking eight league successes for himself. Hansen eventually retired in March 1991. His final game had been in the previous season on April 28th, 1990 at the age of 34.

Accomplishments

In a glittering career, Hansen won eight league titles, three European Cups, two FA Cups, four League Cups, the UEFA Super Cup, and the Charity Shield six times, with Liverpool. He spent 13 seasons at the club, playing in 620 games, including 434 league games. He scored 14 times. He also won the Scottish First Division (second tier) with Partick Thistle. He represented the Scotland national team 26 times. He played for the Scots in the 1982 World Cup. In 2006, Hansen was inducted into the English Football Hall of Fame, and in 2007 he was honoured with the Scottish Hall of Fame. After retiring, Hansen became a well-known pundit and analyst on the BBC television programme, Match of the Day. He worked there for 22 years commenting on the football matches, in particular the defensive play of teams. His final show came in May 2014. He also worked in various forms of the media including radio, Sky TV, and a daily newspaper.

Summary: Alan Hansen was one of the best defenders to have played for Liverpool, and was known for his rational and calm way of thinking. He is an avid golfer, competing with celebrities for charity, and appeared in television adverts.

EMLYN HUGHES

Born: 28th August 1947
Liverpool Debut: 1967
Nationality: English
Position: Defender/Midfielder
Height: 5ft 10in (1.79m)
Major Trophies: 13

Early Career

Emlyn Walter Hughes was born in the town of Barrow-in-Furness, Lancashire (now Cumbria), the son of a professional rugby league player. He played schoolboy football before playing for the youth team in Blackpool. He signed for First Division side Blackpool in 1964 and played for them 28 times before moving to Liverpool in 1967. Legend has it that manager Bill Shankly was stopped in his car by the police as he drove Hughes to Liverpool for the first time and said "Don't you know who I've got in this car? The captain of England!" The policeman peered through the window and said that he didn't recognise the man, to which Shankly replied: "No, but you will!". Hughes did indeed go on to captain his country. He made his debut in March 1967 and scored his first competitive goal five months later. He settled into the midfield role and filled in defensively as he failed to win a trophy in his first four seasons at the club.

Later Career

He had to wait until 1973 to win his first League title with the club, as well as a UEFA Cup triumph. He scored two goals against Merseyside rivals Everton in March and was named captain having told Shankly to strip Tommy Smith of the armband and give it to someone younger. When Liverpool won the FA Cup final in 1974, Hughes received the trophy from the Princess Royal, The Princess Anne. He was soon to be named captain of England. 1976 saw two more trophies attained, before being named Footballer of the Year by the Writers' Association soon after the team's first European Cup success in 1977. Hughes hoisted the European Cup trophy for a second successive year, but made fewer appearances the following season, going on to play his final game against Manchester United in the semi-final of the 1979 FA Cup on April 4th. He was sold to Wolverhampton Wanderers for £90,000 in 1979 and went on to lift the League Cup trophy in his first season there. Further moves to Rotherham United (as player-manager), Hull City, and Mansfield Town followed, before playing the last game of his career during the 1983/84 season with Swansea City.

Accomplishments

Hughes played a total of 665 games for Liverpool, with 474 in the League, during his 13 seasons with the club. He scored 49 goals. For six seasons between 1971/72 and 1976/77 he missed just two league games. The list of titles included four League championships, two European Cups, two UEFA Cups, one FA Cup, and three Charity Shields while with Liverpool, and a League Cup triumph with Wolves. He appeared for the England national team 62 times, 23 as captain. He won the most caps by an England player competing during the '70s but is England's most capped player never to feature in a major finals. After football, he pursued a career in the media as well as doing punditry work. A statue was put up in his home town of Barrow-in-Furness in 2008.

Summary: Hughes was one of the great Liverpool players of the super successful team in the 1970s. He received an OBE in 1980 and was inducted into the National Football Museum's Hall of Fame in 2008.

ROGER HUNT

Born: 20th July 1938
Liverpool Debut: 1959
Nationality: English
Position: Forward
Height: 5 ft 9 in (1.75 m)
Major Trophies: 7

Early Career

Roger Hunt was born in the small village of Glazebury, Lancashire (now Cheshire), and played for non-league Stockton Heath and Devizes Town after leaving school. He was signed by Second Division Liverpool in 1958 and made his debut in September 1959 scoring his first goal against Scunthorpe United. Despite an exodus of players after the arrival of Bill Shankly, Hunt helped Liverpool gain promotion to the First Division in 1962. During that 1961/62 season, he scored 41 goals in 41 league games including five hat-tricks.

Later Career

Hunt's goal scoring continued into the next four seasons as Liverpool won a couple of League titles in 1963/64 and 1965/66. He recorded 31 league goals in 41 games, and 29 in 37 games, in those two seasons. He also scored the first-ever goal seen on the BBC football programme, Match of the Day, in 1964. Hunt was to be the top scorer for the club in eight successive seasons. In 1965, he struck four times as Liverpool reached the FA Cup final and chalked up one of the goals in extra time as his team emerged victorious. His 242nd goal for the club in November 1967, gave him the record as Liverpool's top goalscorer of all-time. His mark of reaching 100 league goals in 152 appearances was a record until broken by Mo Salah in 2021. He played his final match for the team in December 1969. He moved to Bolton Wanderers in 1969 and played for three seasons including a short loan spell in South Africa. He retired in 1972 and was honoured with a testimonial at Anfield with well over 50,000 in attendance.

Accomplishments

Hunt played for 11 seasons with Liverpool, eight in the first division, and scored a record-breaking 285 goals in 492 games, with 244 of them in the league in 404 appearances, a club record, and 44 in the FA Cup. Throughout his career, he scored 309 goals in 568 matches. He won the First Division League title twice, the FA Cup once, and the Charity Shield three times. One of the greatest moments of his career came when he was part of the England team that won the 1966 World Cup. Played on home soil, Hunt played in all six games for England in the tournament, and scored three goals in total, including two against France in the group stage. He then played up front alongside Geoff Hurst in the final, as England clinched the title against West Germany in extra-time with Hurst netting a famous hat-trick. In all, Hunt represented England 34 times and scored 18 goals. He was honoured with an MBE in 2000 for his World Cup triumph. He was inducted into the English Football Hall of Fame in 2006.

Summary: Roger Hunt was one of Liverpool's greatest ever goal scorers, holding numerous records, and one of the best seen in English league football. After retiring, Hunt joined the family-run haulage business. He passed away in September 2021.

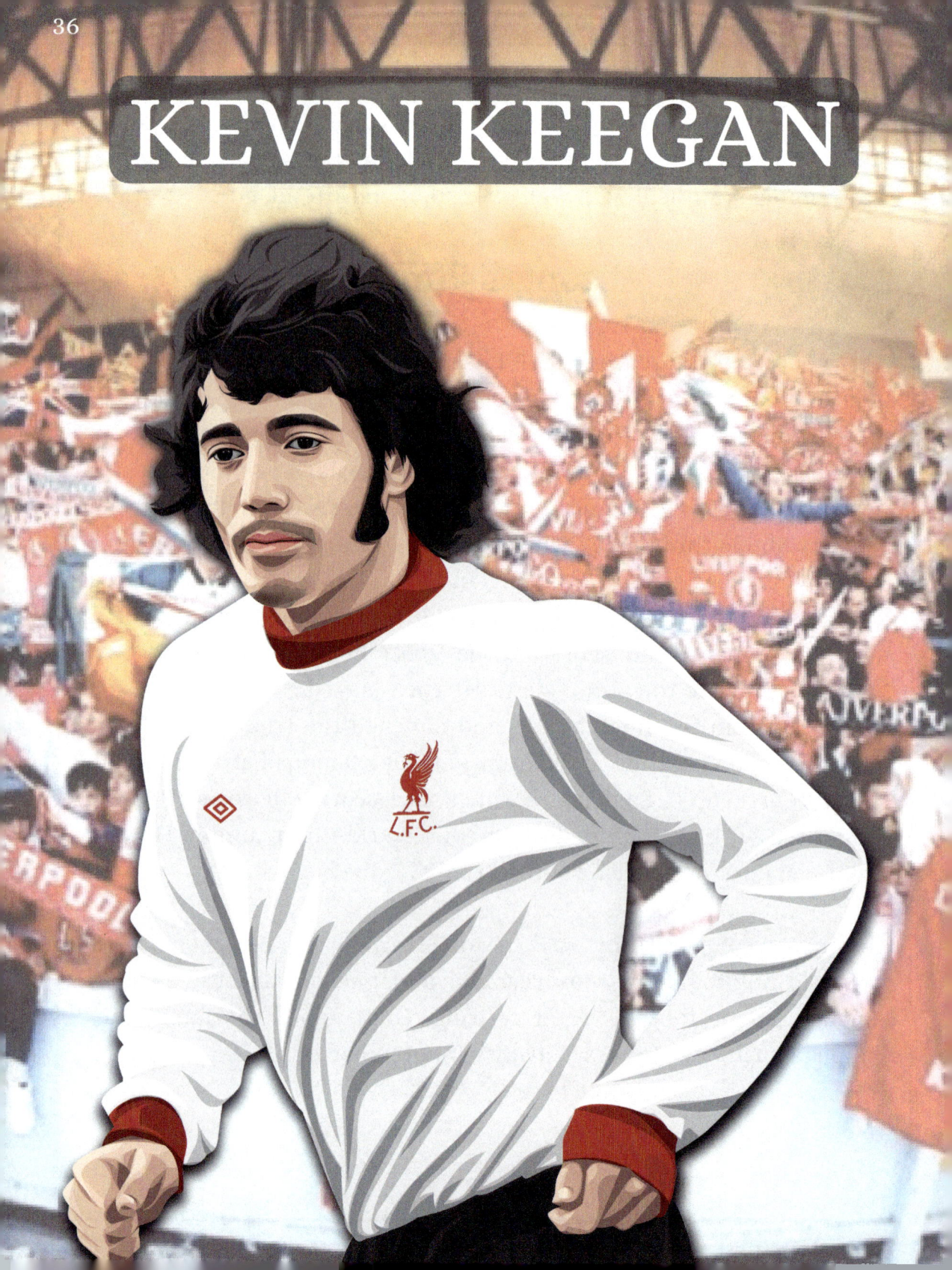

KEVIN KEEGAN

Born: 14th February 1951
Liverpool Debut: 1971
Nationality: English
Position: Forward
Height: 5 ft 8 in (1.73 m)
Major Trophies: 9

Early Career

Joseph Kevin Keegan was born in the village of Armthorpe, in Doncaster, Yorkshire. He was a supporter of local team Doncaster Rovers and had a trial with Coventry City as a schoolboy. He participated in various sports at school before working as an office clerk after leaving. He continued playing for his local youth club, whereupon an opportunity came for him to join Fourth Division side Scunthorpe United in 1968. After making his debut aged just 17, he went on to play all 46 league games in the 1969/70 season. After his third season with the team, an offer came in from First Division side Liverpool and he joined the club in 1971 at the age of 20. Keegan made his debut in August 1971 and scored after only 12 minutes.

Later Career

He won his first major trophy in the 1972/73 season when Liverpool won their eighth League title, scoring a crucial goal in the penultimate game. He also scored two goals in the first leg of the UEFA Cup final triumph in 1973. In the 1974 FA Cup final, Keegan scored with a volley and then a close-range effort, as Liverpool came out victorious. He then helped his team to a League and UEFA Cup double in 1975/76, scoring in both legs of the European final. The 1977 European Cup final on 25th May turned out to be a momentous one for Keegan, and also his final appearance for the team. After spending six seasons at Anfield he moved overseas, securing a record £500,000 deal with West German team Hamburger SV. The side won its first Bundesliga title in 19 years in 1978/79 and reached the final of the 1980 European Cup in the three seasons that Keegan was there. He picked up two consecutive European Footballer of the Year awards. From there, Keegan made a surprise move to Southampton after Liverpool had rejected the chance to re-sign him. He enjoyed his best scoring years with 30 goals in 48 games in 1981/82, and 27 league goals in 41 games in 1983/84. After two seasons he joined Newcastle of the Second Division where he earned legendary status among the fans, clinching promotion in his final season. He played his final match, a testimonial, in May 1984. Keegan then took on a long managerial career, coaching teams such as the England national side, Newcastle United, Fulham, and Manchester City. He guided Newcastle to the First Division championship in 1992/93, and then the runners-up spot in the 1995/96 Premier League.

Accomplishments

Keegan spent only six seasons at Liverpool but played in 323 games and scored 100 goals. He triumphed in the League three times, the FA Cup once, the European Cup once, the UEFA Cup twice, and the Charity Shield twice. He won the German championship with Hamburg, the PFA Players' Player of the Year, the Ballon d'Or twice, and was inducted into the English Football Hall of Fame in 2002. He won 63 caps for England, and scored 21 goals, skippering the side 31 times. He was honoured with an OBE in 1982.

Summary: Kevin Keegan was well-known for his dribbling skills and running with the ball at a swift pace. He appeared on many television programmes as a celebrity away from football. He also released a hit single and was famous in the 70s for trendsetting a new haircut, the perm.

RAY KENNEDY

Born: 28th July 1951
Liverpool Debut: 1974
Nationality: English
Position: Midfielder/Forward
Height: 5 ft 11 in (1.80 m)
Major Trophies: 15

Early Career

Raymond Kennedy was born in the small village of Seaton Delaval, Northumberland where he played schoolboy football. He had a brief spell at Port Vale in 1966 but manager Stanley Matthews felt Kennedy was "too slow to be a footballer" and was considered to be too big and clumsy to be a professional. He was released by the club after being told that he would never make it as a professional. After returning home, he played for a junior team, before he was scouted by Arsenal who signed Kennedy as an apprentice and became a professional in 1968. He made his senior debut in September 1969 in a Cup tie, and his maiden goal came five months later.

Later Career

He scored a goal in the two-leg Inter-Cities Fairs Cup final against Belgian side Anderlecht in 1970, to help Arsenal win its first-ever European competition. Kennedy played 41 of the 42 league games in his second season scoring 19 goals, a career-best, as the club won the championship in 1970/71. The side went on to achieve the League and Cup double that season. From there, he was sold to fellow First Division team Liverpool in 1974 (for a club-record £200,00), where he scored after only 22 minutes on his debut. Kennedy then changed positions from a forward to a midfielder, and Liverpool triumphed in the League and the UEFA Cup in 1976. He netted a goal in the two-leg final against Club Brugge in the first match to help the club to an aggregate win in the European final. Four more trophies followed in 1976/77 with Kennedy again scoring in an end-of-season top of the table clash. He competed in 61 games that season. He posted the winning goal in the 1978 League Cup semi-final, and then guided them to a second successive European Cup success with a goal and two assists in the second leg of the semi-final victory, after having lost the first match. During the 1978/79 season, his goal against Derby County was voted the 'Goal of the Season' by Match of the Day. He was named captain for the semi-final of the European Cup in 1981 against Bayern Munich and scored the winning away goal as the club went on to lift the trophy. He made his final appearance for the club in December 1981, having struck in his final league game a week earlier. He then moved to Welsh team Swansea City under former teammate John Toshack before a short spell with Fourth Fivision side Hartlepool United. Kennedy retired after playing his final game in 1985 after a short spell in Cyrpus and local non-league side Ashington.

Accomplishments

With Liverpool, Kennedy won the First Division title five times, the European Cup three times, the UEFA Cup once, and the League Cup once. With Arsenal, there was a First Division and an FA Cup success. He played in a total of 275 league games for Liverpool, scoring 51 times. He netted 53 times in 158 league matches for Arsenal. He represented the England national football team 17 times and scored three goals.

Summary: Ray Kennedy was a versatile player capable of playing as both a forward and a midfielder. Bob Paisley described him as "one of Liverpool's greatest players and probably the most underrated". He passed away in November 2021.

BILLY LIDDELL

Born: 10th January 1922
Liverpool Debut: 1946
Nationality: Scottish
Position: Left Winger
Height: 6ft (1.84m)
Major Trophies: 1

Early Career

William Beveridge Liddell was born in the small village of Townhill, Scotland. His family lived a life of poverty, but it soon became apparent that he had a great talent for football and by the age of 16, he was being looked at by the top football clubs. He signed for Liverpool in 1938 as an amateur and went on to professional terms a year later. A serious injury threatened his career before the Second World War stopped any competitive football. During the war years, Liddell scored 82 goals in 152 matches playing in various football games for the club. His official debut came on the 5th of January 1946 in the FA Cup, and he scored in the 30th minute.

Later Career

His first official league game saw him score two goals in September 1946. Playing 34 games during the season, Liddell helped Liverpool to win their fifth League title in the first full season after the war. He appeared in every game when his side reached the 1950 FA Cup final, and he totalled 19 goals in 40 league games during the 1951/52 season. However, two seasons later the club was relegated to the second division after finishing bottom of the league. Moving to the centre forward position, Liddell notched 30 goals in 40 league games in 1954/55. He took over the captaincy role in 1955/56, and scored 32 goals during the season. In 1957/58, Liddell broke the record for the most matches played by a Liverpool player in history, breaking the record of Elisha Scott, who had played 468 games. He made fewer appearances in the next couple of seasons, but still managed to complete 40 consecutive cup fixtures for the club. In 1959/60, he scored his final goal for the club during a league game in March and played his final league game on 31st August 1960. At the time, he was the oldest to play for the club post-war at the age of 38, as well as being the oldest to score a goal for the club. After 22 years with the side, Liddell was honoured with a testimonial match in September 1960 against an International XI. With an attendance of over 38,000, the game helped raise £6340 for Liddell, with which he used to buy a house.

Accomplishments

Liddell made 492 league appearances for Liverpool, scoring 215 goals, and had an outright record of 534 games with 228 goals. He played in 16 playing seasons with Liverpool. His only success with the club was the First Division championship. For his national team Scotland, he played 29 matches and scored eight goals. He was inducted into the Scottish Football Hall of Fame in 2008.

Summary: Billy Liddell became noted for his strong physique, acceleration, powerful shot, professionalism, and good conduct on the pitch. He was top scorer in eight out of nine seasons from 1949–50 to 1957–58 and a one-club man with his Liverpool career spanning four decades from 1938 to 1961. Such was his influence and popularity at the club, he acquired the contemporary nickname "Liddellpool". In November 2004, Liddell had a commemorative plaque unveiled at Anfield.

TERRY MCDERMOTT

Born: 8th December 1951
Liverpool Debut: 1974
Nationality: English
Position: Midfielder
Height: 5ft 10in (1.78m)
Major Trophies: 16

Early Career

Terence McDermott was born in the town of Kirkby, in Liverpool, and supported the club as a boy. He played schoolboy football but found it difficult to join the big clubs, before being scouted by Third Division Bury whom he joined in 1969. He made his debut in January 1970 aged 18 and took part in the club's biggest victory in their history, when they won 8-0 against Tranmere Rovers. He played 90 games, before moving to First Division Newcastle United in 1973. He spent three seasons with the club and reached the 1974 FA Cup Final which they lost…to Liverpool 3-0. Bill Shankly signed him for his boyhood team just a few months later in November 1974.

Later Career

He made his debut in November 1974 and scored his first goal four months later. He was in and out of the side for the first two seasons but got a more regular role in 1976/77 when Liverpool retained the League title, and he scored the 'goal of the season' against Everton in the FA Cup semi-final. He also scored the opening goal as Liverpool triumphed in the 1977 European Cup Final, before netting a hat-trick in the UEFA Super Cup final in December. A second European Cup success followed the season after, before a league game in September 1978 saw McDermott score one of the club's finest goals in their history. After running almost the entire length of the pitch from defence, he latched on to a one-touch cross to head into the Tottenham Hotspur net to clinch a 7-0 win. He became the first player to win both the PFA Players' Player of the Year and the Football Writers' Footballer of the Year award in the same season in 1980 after his team had just retained the First Division title. A superb lob-volley in a FA Cup match in 1980, again against Spurs, was another highlight for him in a career littered with spectacular goals. McDermott was in the team when Liverpool won two trophies in 1981, and two more the following season. However, he played his final game for the club in September 1982 in a European Cup tie, before moving back to Newcastle United. He helped the Magpies to promotion back to the First Division in 1984 alongside Kevin Keegan. He then moved to Irish side Cork City, and finally to Cypriot team APOEL, whom he guided to the First Division championship title. McDermott went on to become assistant manager at Newcastle United, whom he helped to second spot in the Premier League in 1996, Celtic, Huddersfield Town, and Birmingham City.

Accomplishments

While at Liverpool, McDermott won four League titles, three European Cups, one UEFA Cup, two League Cups, and four Charity Shields. He played 329 times for the club, 232 in the league, and scored 81 goals. For England, he played 25 games and scored three goals, being included in the squad for two major tournaments.

Summary: Terry McDermott was a strong player full of stamina and ability, capable of scoring some astounding goals from his midfield position. He was assistant manager to fellow Liverpool greats, Kevin Keegan, Kenny Dalglish and John Barnes in the 90s and 2000s.

STEVE MCMANAMAN

Born: 11th February 1972
Liverpool Debut: 1990
Nationality: English
Position: Winger
Height: 6 ft 0 in (1.83 m)
Major Trophies: 2

Early Career

Born in the Bootle area of Liverpool, Steven McManaman was an Everton supporter in his boyhood. Excelling in school football, he was offered a position at fellow Merseyside team Liverpool in 1986, at the age of 14. After progressing through the youth ranks, he made his first-team debut in December 1990. His maiden goal came eight months later. In 1991/92 he played 51 times in his first full season, having just turned 20. He was Man of the Match when Liverpool won the 1992 FA Cup Final against Sunderland, having set up the winner for Michael Thomas. In 1990, McManaman made history by becoming the first player without first-team experience to play for the England under-21 team.

Later Career

He was given a more central midfield role in 1994/95 and started to impress further with his dribbling and running skills. This in turn led to Liverpool winning the League Cup, with McManaman scoring two goals in the final and picking up another Man of the Match prize. He topped the assists charts in 1995/96 with 25 over the season and was a regular recipient of Man of the Match awards over the next two years. He had his best scoring season in 1997/98 with 11 goals in 36 Premier League matches. He also became one of the first modern-day players to write a weekly column for a daily newspaper. Barcelona relentlessly tried to lure him to Spain in the 1990s and there was a bid from Juventus. McManaman was offered the captaincy role at the beginning of the 1997/98 season, but after some time he eventually moved to Real Madrid in 1999 on a Bosman (free transfer). His farewell game for Liverpool came in May 1999. He made a record number of appearances in the Premier League for the club at the time and had a superb record of 112 assists in 272 league appearances. The move to Real made him the highest-paid British footballer, and he gained success instantly with a stunning volley in the 2000 Champions League final triumph. This was followed by a La Liga league success the following season, and two more honours came, before ending his four-year stint at the club. A further move followed to Premier League side Manchester City under Kevin Keegan alongside former teammates Robbie Fowler, Nicolas Anelka, and later, David James, but he failed to score in the two seasons there. His time at City was considered a disappointment and he retired in 2005.

Accomplishments

In nine seasons with Liverpool, McManaman played a total of 364 games for the club scoring 66 goals. His successes included an FA Cup and a League Cup. In four seasons with Real Madrid, he played 158 times and won the La Liga twice, and the Champions League twice. Altogether, he won seven trophies and took part in 11 cup finals with the club. He had the enviable record of 182 assists, including 142 with Liverpool during his career. With England, he appeared 37 times, notching three goals.

Summary: Steve McManaman was praised for his quick running and control skills and provided many chances and assists to his teammates. After retiring, he starred in a film, owned racehorses, did some media work, got involved in corporate work, and was an ambassador for UEFA.

PHIL NEAL

Born: 20th February 1951
Liverpool Debut: 1974
Nationality: English
Position: Full back/Defender
Height: 5 ft 11 in (1.80m)
Major Trophies: 23

Early Career

Philip George Neal was born in the small village of Irchester, in Northamptonshire and played for non-league Wellingborough Town before signing for Northampton Town in 1968, aged just 17. He became a regular in the team from the 1971/72 season onward and stayed there for seven seasons playing 187 games. In 1974, he was signed up by First Division side Liverpool and made his debut in the Merseyside derby against Everton in November, before scoring his maiden goal a year later. The 1975/76 season saw Liverpool win two trophies with Neal playing a full league schedule.

Later Career

After reverting to the right-back position in defence, he scored one of the goals that helped his side beat Borussia Monchengladbach in the 1977 European Cup final, having already scored two in the semi-final. Playing with a strong defence, Neal was part of the Liverpool team that only conceded 16 goals during the 1978/79 league title triumph. A third European Cup success was achieved in 1980/81. As Neal became one of the more senior players, he guided the team to four more championships in two seasons, including two League titles. With a new manager, Neal became the most successful player in Liverpool history in terms of trophies, when a fourth European Cup and a fourth consecutive League Cup were captured in 1983/84. He scored in the European final against AS Roma and took over the captaincy of the club. He played his final game for the club in November 1985. Neal made an incredible 365 successive league appearances between December 1974 and September 1983 and played a total of 417 consecutive matches for the club between October 1976 and September 1983, a record. In eight consecutive seasons he played in every single league game and missed one league game in 10. After 11 years at the club, he joined Bolton Wanderers as a player-manager before retiring in 1989. He also had managerial stints at Coventry City, Cardiff City, Manchester City, and worked as an assistant coach to the English national team.

Accomplishments

In an incredible career, Neal won eight League titles, four European Cups, one UEFA Cup, four League Cups, and five Charity Shields with Liverpool. He played 650 games for Liverpool in 12 seasons, including 455 appearances in the league. He scored a total of 59 goals for the club. A total career tallied up to 901 games. As manager of Bolton Wanderers, he won the Football League Trophy. He won 50 caps for England, scoring five times. He has worked as a football pundit on television and radio and written two autobiographies.

Summary: Phil Neal is one of the most successful players in history in terms of trophies won playing association football; a fantastic 23 while playing for Liverpool. Out of the nine European Cup/Champions League finals that Liverpool has contested only Neal has scored in more than one of them. His nickname at Liverpool was Zico in reference to the great Brazilian playmaker of the time.

MICHAEL OWEN

Born: 14th December 1979
Liverpool Debut: 1997
Nationality: English
Position: Striker
Height: 5 ft 8 in (1.73 m)
Major Trophies: 6

Early Career

Born in the city of Chester, Cheshire, Michael James Owen started playing football at an early age, and by the age of ten was being scouted, having scored a record-breaking 97 goals in a single season competing for his school. His father was a professional footballer. The big English clubs had an interest in Owen, but despite being an Everton fan it was Liverpool who impressed him the most and he signed up with the youth team. He proceeded to break scoring records while also representing the England youth teams. He went on to score a goal on his debut in May 1997 aged just 17.

Later Career

The 1997/98 saw a host of accolades with the league's Golden Boot and the Young Player of the Year award, as well as coming second in the World Player of the Year category. Injuries hindered him for a while, before helping Liverpool achieve a trio of trophies in the 2000/01 season. He scored 24 goals during the season, including two late goals in the FA Cup triumph. He was voted the European Player of the Year. His goal ratio upped to a career-best 28 goals in 43 games the following season, as his club finished runners-up in the league, including the 100th goal of his career. Interest was shown by Spanish side Real Madrid, but Owen continued to perform, including his 100th Premier League goal, and a late strike in the 2003 League Cup Final success. He led Liverpool to a place in the 2004/05 Champions League but duly moved to Real Madrid in August 2004 for £8 million. He played with a host of stars, including David Beckham and Luis Figo, and ended his debut season with 13 goals in 36 league games. However, after a year, he was snapped up by Newcastle United for £16.8m, having been linked with Liverpool and Everton, and stayed there for four seasons, suffering several injuries along the way. His next move came as a surprise and was rather controversial…to Manchester United. He played sporadically over the next three seasons but did get his first Premier League title. Owen took the final step in his playing career by signing for Stoke City in 2012, before playing his farewell match on the 19th of May 2013, having been plagued by numerous injuries in the preceding years.

Accomplishments

For Liverpool, Owen made 216 Premier League appearances scoring 118 goals in eight seasons. In total, he netted 158 goals in 297 games. Across his career, he scored 222 goals in 482 appearances. The honours at Liverpool included an FA Cup, the UEFA Cup, and two League Cups. With Manchester United, he secured a Premier League and League Cup success. He won the BBC Sports Personality of the Year in 1998, the Ballon d'Or in 2001, and was inducted into the Hall of Fame for English football in 2014. Owen is England's sixth highest goalscorer of all-time with 40 goals in 89 games, including a memorable solo effort in the 1998 World Cup against Argentina.

Summary: Michael Owen was seen as one of the best strikers of his generation, with swift pace and clinical finishing. His prime was early in his career relative to other players as he was blighted by injuries that affected one of his most key attributes, pace. He owns racehorses and has appeared on television as a football pundit.

BOB PAISLEY

Born: 23rd January 1919
Liverpool Debut: 1939
Nationality: English
Position: Left-half/Midfielder
Major Trophies as Player: 1
Major Trophies as Manager: 20

Early Career

Robert Paisley was born in the small town of Hetton-le-Hole, County Durham, where coal mining was the main way of life. His father was a miner, but life was a struggle due to strikes and a shortage of essentials. Paisley was a superb football player at his school, and he joined top amateur side Bishop Auckland, whom he helped achieve the treble in the 1938/39 season. He signed for Liverpool in 1939, soon after his 20th birthday. Paisley had to wait until January 1946 before making his official first team debut due to the Second World War. Having served in the war, Paisley eventually scored his first goal in May 1948.

Later Career

He helped Liverpool to claim the League title in 1946/47, the club's first success in 24 years. He became a regular in the next few seasons, appearing in 30 or more games in most outings. Having become the club captain in 1950/51, Paisley retired in 1954. He took on the role of team physio, and then a reserve team coach, developing a great working relationship with Bill Shankly when the new manager arrived on the scene in 1959. Liverpool became more of a force throughout the '60s. When Shankly retired unexpectedly in 1974, Paisley was appointed by the directors as his replacement (which he reluctantly accepted) He would lead the Liverpool team to outstanding success for years to come. After a trophy-less first season, Liverpool picked up the League and UEFA Cup titles in 1976. The following season they won their tenth League title, as well as lifting the European Cup for the first time. In a season where Paisley signed both Kenny Dalglish and Graeme Souness, Liverpool were runners-up in the league, but retained the prestigious European Cup, as well as winning the European Super Cup. The club's 11th League title in 1978/79 was acquired with a record 68 points and only 16 goals conceded. The next four seasons saw Paisley guide the team to three more League titles, a third European Cup success, and three successive League Cups. The 1982/83 season was Bob Paisley's final year as manager. In nine years, there were six League titles (runners-up twice), three European Cups, three League Cups, one European Super Cup, one UEFA Cup, and six Charity Shields. An incredible 20 trophies make him one of the most successful English club football managers of all-time.

Accomplishments

Apart from the stack of titles, Paisley was named Manager of the Year six times, and entered both the English and European Halls of Fame. As a manager, he won 308 games out of 535 matches, and in the League managed in 378 matches, winning 212. He was the subject of the television programme 'This Is Your Life' in 1977, and a statue was erected in his honour in January 2020 outside the home of Liverpool football club, Anfield.

Summary: Bob Paisley was one of the greatest managers of all-time, and possibly the best seen in British football. He spent 44 years at Anfield and was awarded the OBE in 1983. Paisley passed away in 1996 at the age of 77.

IAN RUSH

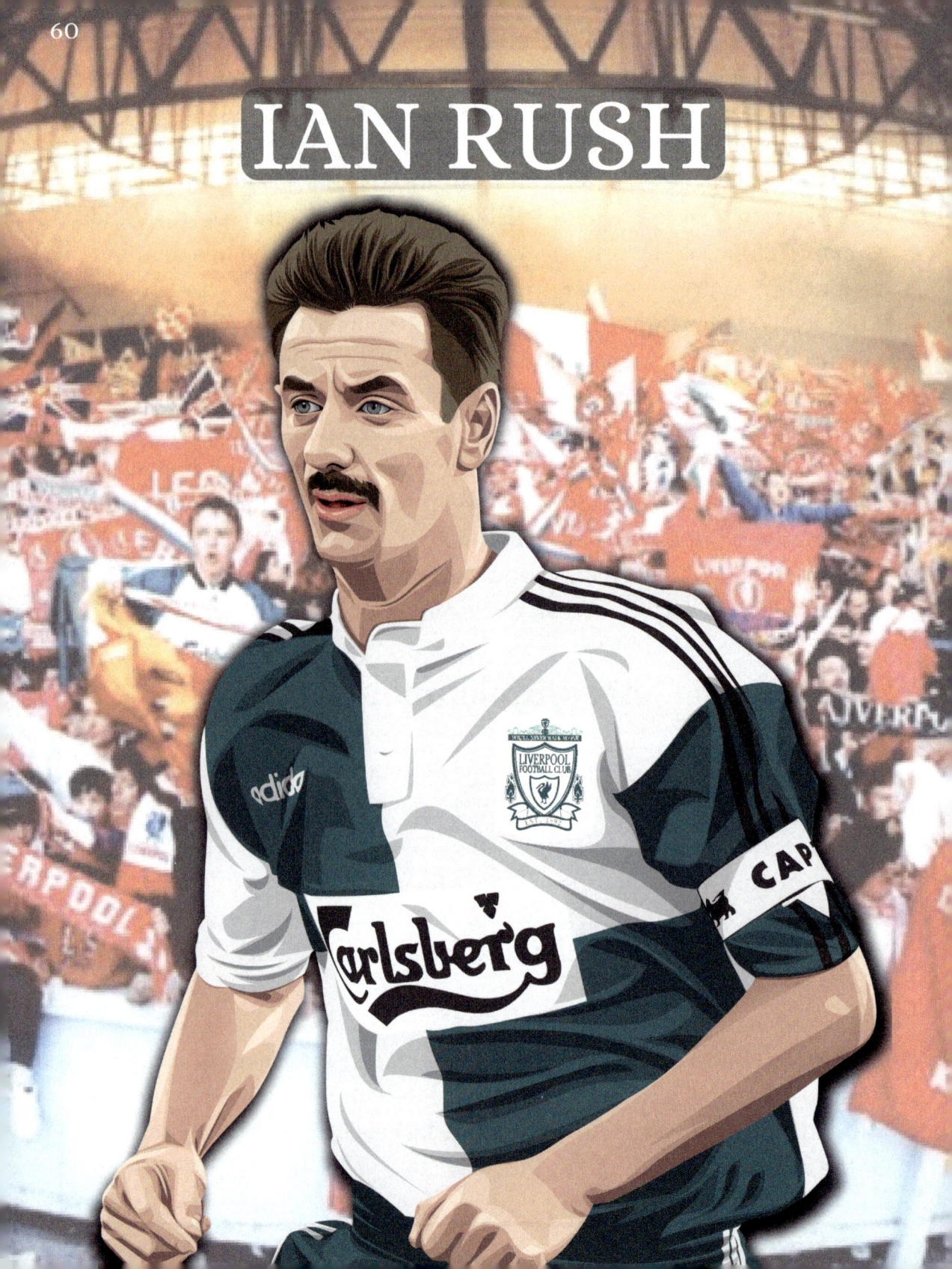

Born: 20th October 1961
Liverpool Debut: 1980
Nationality: Welsh
Position: Forward
Height: 5 ft 11 in (1.80 m)
Major Trophies: 20

Early Career

Ian James Rush was born in the small city of St. Asaph, Flintshire, in Wales into a large family and supported Everton. He impressed scouts at the early age of 13 playing for his school. He had trials at several clubs and eventually joined English side Chester City, where he stayed for two years before more interest saw Liverpool snap him up at the age of 19 for £300,000 - a record for a teenager at the time. Rush made his debut in a Reds shirt in December 1980 but spent most of his first season playing in the reserves, and had to wait until September 1981 to score his first goal, which he did in a European Cup tie. He soon started to score in a succession of games in early 1982, as Liverpool climbed from mid table to the top of the League, and he ended the season with a personal tally of 30 goals in 49 games.

Later Career

By helping Liverpool to their second successive League title, Rush was voted the Young Player of the Year by the PFA in 1983, for his 24 league goals including a quadruple against Everton in the Merseyside derby. More accolades followed in 1984, with Liverpool completing a historic treble. Rush scored an amazing 47 goals in 65 games in all competitions during that season. The 1985/86 season saw Rush net two goals in the FA Cup final victory over Everton, picking up the

Man of the Match award in the process. With the club banned from entering European competition, Rush received interest from elsewhere and eventually he decided to sign for Italian side Juventus for a British record £3.2 million in 1986. He spent a season on loan at Liverpool before moving to Italy. He ended the 1986/87 English season with 30 league goals. His time at Juventus was less successful as he struggled to integrate himself in the dressing room and adapt to the Italian style of play. He returned to the Reds in 1988 and scored twice again against Everton in the 1989 FA Cup Final win. His 18 goals in 36 games saw Liverpool secure another League title in 1989/90, and he was a regular scorer in the following campaign. He finished the top scorer for the team in two successive seasons, but his long career at the Anfield club came to an end in 1996, when he played in the FA Cup Final. He had brief stints with other clubs, including Leeds United, Newcastle United and Australian side, Sydney Olympic, before finally calling it a day in 1999 aged 38.

Accomplishments

In an illustrious career, Rush played a total of 660 games for Liverpool scoring 346 times, a club record, with 229 of them in 469 league games. He spent 15 seasons at the club. In that time, he was victorious in the League five times, the European Cup twice, the FA Cup three times, and the League Cup five times. He was top scorer for the club in eight seasons. For his national team Wales, he scored a record 28 goals in 73 games.

Summary: Ian Rush is the greatest goal scorer in Liverpool football club history, who also impressed with his defensive work. Since retiring he had a short spell as a manager and worked on television as a football pundit.

TOMMY SMITH

Born: 5th April 1945
Liverpool Debut: 1963
Nationality: English
Position: Defender
Height: 5 ft 10 in (1.78 m)
Major Trophies: 14

Early Career

Thomas Smith was born in Liverpool where he joined the club as a member of the ground staff and became a schoolboy player as a centre-forward. He turned professional in 1962 and played his first game in May 1963. However, he had to wait until August 1964 for his next match and his first goal for the club. He played as a defender in a European Cup tie but was used mostly in midfield. He took part in every single game in the 1965 FA Cup run, as Liverpool won the trophy for the first time.

Later Career

Smith appeared in all 42 league games as his side won the title in 1966. The 1966 Charity Shield would be his last trophy until the 1972/73 League and the UEFA Cup double. During that time, in 1970, he was awarded the captaincy leading his team to the 1971 FA Cup Final. He nearly left the club after losing his preferred centre-back position and the captaincy to Emlyn Hughes but ended up staying and later assisted two goals when Liverpool beat Newcastle to win the 1974 FA Cup. He played a valuable role as Liverpool achieved another double in 1976, including both legs of the UEFA Cup Final. Away from Liverpool, Smith played in the United States for Tampa Bay Rowdies on loan, during the summer of '76 where he was nicknamed 'The Tank' due to his toughness. With fewer appearances for the team, Smith still managed to play out the 1976/77 season as the club retained the league title, and then played a pivotal role in the 1977 European Cup Final, when his second-half header gave Liverpool the lead, on route to a momentous victory. This was Smith's eighth goal in European competition. He was honoured with a testimonial game soon after. He played one more season for Liverpool and played his farewell game on the 25th of April 1978. He spent more time in the US, this time with the Los Angeles Aztecs, some of it coaching, before joining Swansea City in 1978. He helped them to promotion from the Third Division, and eventually retired in 1979.

Accomplishments

Smith played a total of 638 games for Liverpool with 467 of them in the League, and 85 in European club competition. His career total came to 710 matches and 50 goals. He spent 16 seasons at Anfield. With Liverpool he was victorious in the league four times, the European Cup once, the FA Cup twice, the UEFA Cup twice, and the Charity Shield four times. For the England national team, he played just once, in 1971. He was honoured with an MBE in 1978 for services to football.

Summary: Tommy Smith was a tough and fearless player. Described as hard and intimidating by his fellow players, his main position was as a central defender, even though he fulfilled the midfield role capably on numerous occasions. He spent a short time at Liverpool as a youth coach and wrote a weekly column for the city's daily newspaper. He passed away in April 2019.

GRAEME SOUNESS

Born: 6th May 1953
Liverpool Debut: 1978
Nationality: Scottish
Position: Midfielder
Height: 5 ft 11 in (1.80 m)
Major Trophies: 14 + 1 as manager

Early Career

Born in the capital city of Scotland, Edinburgh, Graeme James Souness was a supporter of Scottish sides Rangers and Hearts. He became a professional with Tottenham Hotspur aged just 15, and had a loan spell with Canadian team, Montreal Olympique. Dismayed at his lack of first team football at Spurs, he moved to Middlesbrough for £30,000 with whom he developed his dogged and hard reputation. A move to Liverpool followed in January 1978 as a replacement for club legend Ian Callaghan, joining the Scottish duo of Kenny Dalglish and Alan Hansen, who had already signed in recent seasons. His first goal came in February and was voted the goal of the season by the fans, and he assisted the winning goal in the 1978 European Cup final.

Later Career

A host of triumphs followed with two League titles and another European Cup success, in three years, before prompting manager Bob Paisley to give the captaincy to Souness in the 1981/82 campaign. Under his leadership, Liverpool won four more trophies in the next two seasons, before the 1983/84 year saw three more accolades, with Souness scoring the winning goal in the League Cup Final, and converting a spot kick in the penalty shoot-out win against Roma in the 1984 European Cup final; his final appearance for the club. After playing in 359 games, Souness finished his career with Liverpool, scoring 55 goals. He moved to Italian side Sampdoria for a short time, before joining Rangers as a player-manager in 1986 at the age of 33. He won the title that season, their first in 8 years, and was able to attract major players from England to sign for the club. He played 50 league games, before finally retiring as a player in 1991 at the age of 38. He played for 20 minutes in his final career game. After Rangers, he managed Liverpool, Galatasaray, Torino, Southampton and Blackburn before his last job for Newcastle whom he left in 2006.

Accomplishments

In seven seasons with Liverpool, Souness won five League titles, three European Cups, and four League Cups. With a variety of clubs, he played a total of 673 games in his career, scoring 92 goals in that time. He won the European Cup Golden Boot award in 1980/81. As manager, he won three league titles and four League Cups at Rangers before winning the FA Cup with Liverpool, the Turkish Cup with Galatasaray and the League Cup with Blackburn Rovers. He played 54 times for Scotland and represented them at three World Cups. Other honours included an induction into the national football team roll of honour, and into both the English and Scottish Halls of Fame.

Summary: Graeme Souness was a tough and gritty footballer, fearless and able to take on all opponents. His hard man image brought home many titles, both as a manager and a player, winning altogether eight major league titles, and representing a dozen different teams throughout his career. An autobiography was written in 1985. He is currently an expert analyst with Sky Sports on television.

LUIS SUÁREZ

Born: 24th January 1987
Liverpool Debut: 2011
Nationality: Uruguayan
Position: Striker
Height: 6 ft (1.82 m)
Major Trophies: 1

Early Career

Luis Alberto Suárez Diaz was born in the city of Salto, Uruguay. When he was a kid, a car ran over his foot, breaking the fifth metatarsal bone. He played his first senior game for Uruguayan side Nacional, whom he helped win the league title in 2005/06. Seen by a group of scouts, he was signed by Dutch club Groningen when aged only 19. Another Dutch club Ajax, then recruited him for the 2007/08 season, and he netted 22 times in 31 league games the following season. As the new captain, he blasted 35 goals in 33 games, 49 in all competitions, during the 2009/10 season. Liverpool then signed him for £22.8 million in January 2011 after Fernando Torres' shock departure to Chelsea. He requested the famous number 7 shirt and made his debut shortly after against Stoke City in which he scored. He helped Liverpool go from 12th in the league in mid-January to finish sixth that season.

Later Career

In the 2012/13 season, Suárez became the third Liverpool player to score 20 goals in a Premier League season. After initially wanting to leave the club that summer, he reversed his decision and went on to brake Robbie Fowler's club record of most goals in a Premier League season by scoring an incredible 31 goals in 33 league games as Liverpool agonisingly finished second in the league. In December 2013, he became the first player in Premier League history to score three hat-tricks against the same club, Norwich, and took his scoring record against them to 11 goals in 5 matches. He was the League's top scorer and won the Premier League Player of the Season for his efforts - becoming the first non-European to do so. He shared the European Golden boot that year with Cristiano Ronaldo. Suárez moved to Barcelona in July 2014 for £65m where he confirmed his place as one of the best strikers in the world. He bagged 25 goals in his inaugural season, including a goal in the Champions League Final, as Barca won the treble. In his first 100 games for the club, Suárez scored 88 times, as another 37 goals came his way in 2016/17, and he notched his 400th career goal the following season. In 2018/19, Suarez scored a memorable hat-trick in the El Clasico against Real Madrid, en route to a fourth La Liga title. In 2020, Suárez left on a free to Atletico Madrid, and guided them to their first La Liga title in seven years in his debut season, while scoring his 500th career goal along the way.

Accomplishments

In a Liverpool shirt, Suárez played 133 times, and scored 82 goals, winning the League Cup once. He had a more prosperous time at Barcelona, starting in 283 games and grabbing 198 goals, including 147 goals in 191 league matches. He won four league titles and one Champions League title while he was there. He is Uruguay's record goalscorer with 68 goals in 130 caps and helped his team to the 2010 World Cup semi-finals and won the 2011 Copa America.

Summary: Luis Suárez is a prolific goal scorer and is considered one of the greatest strikers of all-time. Able to score from anywhere with accurate shooting, he is also a great provider to other teammates. However, Suarez has been involved in many controversies throughout his career which has somewhat tarnished his reputation but nevertheless, he has been an outstanding player.

PHIL THOMPSON

Born: 21st January 1954
Liverpool Debut: 1971
Nationality: English
Position: Centre back/Defender
Height: 6ft (1.83m)
Major Trophies: 23

Early Career

Philip Bernard Thompson was born in Kirkby, 6 miles from Liverpool. He was a Liverpool supporter growing up and stood on the Kop as a boy. He joined the club as an apprentice where he captained the youth team playing in midfield. A day after his 17th birthday, he became a professional and made his debut a year later in April 1972 versus Manchester United. He moved from midfield to central defence, the season after seeing his side achieve the double in 1972/73. He was instrumental in man-marking striker Malcolm Macdonald when Liverpool triumphed in the 1974 FA Cup final by easily defeating Newcastle United.

Later Career

Thompson missed just one league game and scored in the semi-final of the UEFA Cup, as Liverpool achieved another double in 1975/76. He missed the 1977 European Cup triumph due to injury, but won a third league title, before being the saviour in the '78 European Cup Final when he cleared off the goal line to enable his team to clinch the trophy by a single goal. He missed just three games when Liverpool picked up the League title in 1979 and was made captain soon after. He then played in all the league matches when the title was successfully defended the following season. One of the proudest moments of his career came when he collected the trophy as skipper, when the club claimed their third European Cup prize in 1981. Two more league championships followed in 1982 and 1983 taking his tally to seven. But with age catching up he competed in his final game for the club in August 1983 against Manchester United in the Charity Shield at Wembley. He moved to Second Division Sheffield United in 1985 and played 37 games for the club before retiring at the age of 31. He returned to Anfield in 1986 as an assistant team coach and helped guide the club to two more League titles in 1988 and 1990 plus the FA Cup in 1989. He left the club in 1992 after a spat with manager Graeme Souness but returned as assistant to Gerard Houllier in 1998 and was part of the 2000/01 treble season. He had a brief spell as caretaker manager when Houllier fell ill in the early 2000s but still managed to scoop two Manager of the Month awards.

Accomplishments

Thompson appeared in 477 matches for Liverpool in 13 seasons, and 340 times in the league. He scored a total of 13 goals. He won the League seven times, the European Cup twice, the UEFA Cup twice, the FA Cup once, the League Cup twice, and the Charity Shield six times. He played 42 times for the England national team, scoring once, and was skipper for six matches.

Summary: Phil Thompson was one of the most successful players in the club's history. He was known for his professionalism and reliability. After retiring, apart from coaching, Thompson was a well-known expert and pundit on Sky Sports on their weekly flagship show, Soccer Saturday. He worked there for 22 years. He also helps students at the University of Liverpool with their football studies with his lectures and guidance.

FERNANDO TORRES

Born: 20th March 1984

Liverpool Debut: 2007

Nationality: Spanish

Position: Striker

Height: 6 ft 1 in (1.86 m)

Major Trophies: 0

Early Career

Fernando José Torres Sanz was born in the city of Fuenlabrada just outside of Madrid. He began as a goalkeeper but became a striker, once scoring 55 goals in a season playing for a youth team. He joined Atletico Madrid's youth team aged 11 in 1995. He made his first team debut in May 2001 before scoring his first goal a week later. He netted 13 goals in 29 league games when Atletico were promoted to the top flight in 2002/03. He scored 19 times in 35 league outings the following season, before being named as club captain aged just 19.

Later Career

He signed for Liverpool in 2007 for around £20m. He scored his first league goal a week after his debut, and his first hat-trick a month later. By March, he had completed three hat-tricks for the club, and by the end of the season Torres had scored 33 goals in 46 games, including 24 in 33 in the Premier League, a record for a foreign player in his inaugural English season. The goal scoring continued, including the 1000th goal by a Liverpool player in the Premier League, and his 50th for the club in just 84 appearances. He was named in a World XI and came third in the FIFA World Player of the Year. In 2009/10 he recorded the fastest to 50 league goals by a Liverpool player and ended the season with 22 goals in 32 games, the team's top scorer. In January 2011, he made a shock move to Chelsea for a British transfer record fee of around £50 million to the anger of the Liverpool supporters. He was far less clinical with Chelsea scoring just 45 goals in 172 games for them but did win four trophies including the Champions League. After spending four months at Italian Serie A side AC Milan, Torres moved back to Atletico Madrid on loan and scored his 100th goal for the club, before winning his first trophy with his boyhood club, the 2018 Europa League. A short stint followed with Japanese side Sagan Tosu before retiring in 2019.

Accomplishments

Four seasons at Liverpool saw Torres score 65 league goals in 102 games, while his record at Atletico Madrid was 109 league goals in 321 appearances. Torres was hugely successful at international level, winning the 2010 World Cup and the European Championships in 2008 and 2012, being named Man of the Match in the 2008 final. He is the only player to score in two European Championship Finals and scored 38 goals in 110 caps. He was honoured with the Spanish Royal Order of Sports Merit.

Summary: Torres was known for his supreme pace and finishing and in his prime was one of the deadliest strikers in world football. Despite his controversial move to Chelsea, he still gave the Anfield faithful many great moments despite not winning a trophy.

You have now come to the end of the book, I really hope you have enjoyed it and have learnt lots of awesome facts about these Liverpool FC legends to impress your mates and family.

As a small independent publisher, positive reviews left on our books go a long way to attracting new readers who share your passion for the game.

If you are able to take a few minutes out of your day to leave a review it would be greatly appreciated!

If you spot any issues you would like to raise, please do **email me before leaving a negative review** with any comments you may have.

I will be more than happy to liaise with you and can offer refunds or updated copies if you are unhappy with your purchase.

kieran.brown2402@gmail.com